Poems and Essays

by Leon Davis

authorHOUSE®

AuthorHouse™
1663 Liberty Drive
Bloomington, IN 47403
www.authorhouse.com
Phone: 833-262-8899

Published by AuthorHouse 10/18/2023

ISBN: 979-8-8230-1638-4 (sc)
ISBN: 979-8-8230-1637-7 (e)

Library of Congress Control Number: 2023920092

Print information available on the last page.

This book is printed on acid-free paper.

Contents

See it through

Don't start something and don't see it through,
Never begin an act, and no complete it
Never start something, and not see it through
Any act works starting should be seen
through until the end is finished
Let start over with a new beginning
Before I let us break up,
let me see you through
Let our beginning be forever getting
Deeper as the sea,
Forever it will be, brighter than the
Brightest star,
Forever getting brighter than the
Brightest star,
This is truly who we are,
The endless feeling for you,
I carry in my heart
My love for a, mother dear.

The way it Goes

The best thought out place go bad
The happiest day next day is sad,
The darkest night next day is good
The emptiest day, the night is bright,
Joy and happiness are brothers
One day joy rules, the next day sadness rules,
Nothing is all one thing, life
is full of contradiction,
Sometimes good is all we see,
Yet sorrow will take its turn,
Joy will be yours tomorrow,
So always look for the good in everything,
Somewhere you'll see bad and good whatever comes,
Think of happy times, when sadness
Seems so near, and your tears
will wash away all the sad times,
Tomorrow joy will surely shine

My Twin

Elaine–Nefertarie
The queen I lost in
My youth–kinship
Destroyed our love,
Life as taken me
Down many lovely roads,
I went to my real struggle
To gain fame and wealth
To attract my Queen back to me
Amenra help me to be
Strong and determine in
This my new endeavor,
I love thee Oh Amenra
The god of our father and mother
Praying for I need thee oh Amenra.

Why we wait

Man life is short and hard,
But the good times come and go fast,
When the end is near it only seems like a slow time,
Yet our day has come when we realize who we are,
The past cannot control the future,
Change is always possible,
What you make of every moment
is paid in the future present sweetness,
Never yesterday but always today.

Where's It At

The stolen kingdom of Africa,
Sits in the midst of the,
American empire,
They came in chains,
And was forced to do the labor for greedy capitalists,
Stolen was the culture and language of people,
Who had known many seasons,
People that had developed the theory of monotheism,
Those who knew God on a personal and a national basis,
We lost our institutions and became part of one, slavery.

The Underclass

Those who did not make it,
They were left behind in the dying communities,
Communities that depend on the broader society,
A class of individuals who are denied a living,
They only exist from day to day,
Their behavior became negative,
They have no hope of a new home or family,
Their children remain on welfare,
Their women begin to have children from many different men,
The mark of oppression.
Throw off the yoke
Fight and be free

Black Queen

You stand above all the rest,
You are black and beautiful,
Your heart is full of love,
Your soul is pure like a dove,
All you know is love,
Black Queen,
Your voice is heard in the blackest midnight
You love the black man and when he is pure,
You prefer your sun.

Black Christmas

Your beauty is like the night,
Peace and serenity is your soul,
Children are excited because company is here,
Black folk gather and talk about the year,
Your old friends who have lived through the year, are near,
Remembrance of the days of youth,
When your children are playing with the toys,
That x-mas has brought them joy.

King of Mali

O king of Mali,
Hail to the divine one,
African greatness I call forward,
Blessed is the king,
May we all prosper,
Let the God Amen reign supreme,
Amen is the God of the Black Man,
All credit is due to him,
He cares for the black man,
Truly only the weak can't see him.
RA is his daytime name–
RA-AMEN–Now! Now!

Bobby Hutton

You died with your hands on the trigger,
You would meet death instead of prison,
You would live only as a free man,
The courage of a saint that would not bend,
Death to a soldier is the price we pays for glory,
A martyr in our war for human rights,
You would not surrender,
Thou the pigs came so you could not live again,
All you knew is we must fight.

Home Alone

The rain beats upon the glass,
Not forever will the storm last,
The rain falls gently on my window pane,
Lonely is my fate,
I may have discovered too late,
When the cats' away the mouse will play,
The rat laughs at the cat,
When he can see where his hole is at,
I look into the night,
All I see is black.

We Are The Majority

When you look at the whole Earth,
The dark people are the majority,
We are the rightful owners of the Earth,
We are the rightful rulers of the Earth,
Earth is under occupation and rule by a foreigner,
America belongs to the dark man,
South America and North America belong to us,
Asia belongs to us and India, Africa,
We are the majority,
We must teach the white man.

Love Gone By

Each day I see shadows of my love,
Never does my love grow a bud,
Here comes fate with its destiny in a doubt,
And I am left without,
I am here on the outside looking in on love,
While lovers go unaware,
That innocents are there,
Love gone by,
I remember the first kiss upon my lips,
A virgin girl she insist,
Bare of all pretense,
We made love very, very intense,
But love seems to resist my grasp for eternity,
It keeps slipping from my fist.

Baby Come Over

Girl what are you doing today,
Why don't you come over to play,
Let us lay and listen to the lightening,
As we lay in a quiet storm booming,
Baby come over,
Let us make time and fall in love,
As the Gods fight in the heavens above,
Baby come over,
Let us dance to the love songs,
Let our love grow strong.

The Faithful

Oh Allah I love thee, Allah, love my creation,
Oh Allah I love thee, Allah, love my sunshine,
Oh Allah I love thee, Allah, love my rain,
Oh Allah I love thee, Allah, love my people as you love yourself,
Oh Allah I love thee, Allah, love my trees,
Oh Allah I love thee, Allah, love my creation
Oh AmenRa, I love thee
Love my wisdom,
Oh man can you
Retrieve that which
A fly snatches,
What can a man do
When a tornado storms.

Coletrain, the Liberator

A love supreme, a love supreme
The Creator loves all creation,
He never looks on any one man with special favors,
It is up to the Blackman to free himself,
The notions of inferiority are propagated from a white society,
We must ignore its assault on our dignity,
We must take our African-triscity to its logical end,
Culturally Coletrain epitomizes what must be done,
He took Jazz as played from a revolutionary vision,
And stamp upon the psychic of the Blackman and woman
A new level of consciousness.
Blow train blow
Away the chains of oppression.

The Power of Nommo

The word is the conquer tool,
The weapon of these
Who forges new meaning,
From the mouth of babes comes wisdom of the ages,
The ancient one lives in the ruins of past empires,
The word is the truth that rises from the past of falsehood,
Truth comes, and falsehood disappears from the mind of
the people,
Knowledge is the fruit of the word,
Nommo is power
Nommo–the word is plain
How sounds create the
World of mankind,
Nommo is the seed
The fruit is ideas.

Addicted

When a man craves something,
He loses control of his body,
He loses control of his mind,
His urges are rampant, and his will is cripple,
He becomes as a baby helpless before the world,
So many times, he loses that which he loves,
A woman, a friend, a family,
And sometimes he loses his very life,
He is the poorest of the poor.

Words of Castles

Build black man,
Take your life from evil,
The evil of the bottle,
The evil of the pipe,
From the evil of the needle,
Rise up black man,
From the stale breath of crack and tobacco,
From the sleep of heroine,
From the ecstasy of coke,
Build lives of goodness and sacrifice for the children's sake,
Rise up black man,
From the self-hate that deny you your responsibilities,
Rise up from unproductive lives,
To build castle of gold.

At school I get off

What's all the glamour for,
When you finish you go to work,
School is a haven for the child-adult,
The first day you are overwhelmed by the new faces,
In their eyes you see sparkles for greatness,
The hurried activity of young hearts set to find destiny,
The words of giants linger in the atmosphere,
I set out a student of Socrates, Jesus, Mohammed, Krumah,
The great adventure of the modern sciences,
Yet all is left for the growth of the mind,
School is where ideas clash,
And from a fire of stones.
Come wisdom in a book
Wise minds arise,
To take the world
To new heights,
New invention
Ease the plight of mankind.

Self-Accusing Spirit

There is a struggle between good and evil tendencies,
Allah, universal brotherhood,
Practice brotherhood with those of like intent,
Never force yourself on any person male or female,
Let it be mutual affection,
The conscience of man drives him mad,
When it is out of control,
Balance is essential,
To a peaceful mind,
The mind is at rest,
The desire of the sages.

Freedom from

The stench of crack,
The smell of those who don't have time to bathe,
The capture of love itself in the mind of a junkie,
Who steals from his loved ones,
And gives to the exploiter,
And make a brother a traitor,
He has taken the game of the oppressor,
To run it on a sister or brother,
All money ain't good money,
When the destruction of a comrade,
Results as the enrichment of a few dealers,
Who are now partners with the enemy of all.

Where Are The Fathers

Who made this life I see,
Was the woman alone when she conceived,
Where are the fathers?
Has he been denied the right to provide for his offspring,
Are some mothers against a man raising his children,
Has she decided that this life they created,
Belongs only to her,
Has she doubt about love,
And think her child is the only love she can count on,
What about a strong caring father,
Has he vanished with the times,
Consumed by drugs or alcohol,
Or are the mothers anti-black,
And really hate black mankind.
No, the Black woman is
The invisible strength,
She can liberate
The Black Nation-
Move over Black man
And let her be free.

Today I Heard

Today I heard that a black man killed 22 brothers,
I wonder were there more,
The destroyer sent in more troops,
The troops needed only a new excuse to kill,
22 black people died today,
Another day of mourning in South Africa,
The shadow people lie about how many it was,
How long must we suffer oh, Olodumare.

Black Mama

Black Mama! Black Mama,
You look so good,
Black Mama! Black Mama,
I do know you could,
Black Mama! Black Mama,
I'm your tom cat,
Black Mama! Black Mama,
You are so fat,
Black Mama! Black Mama,
I want you in a sack,
Black Mama! Black Mama,
Wow you are stacked,
Black Mama! Black Mama,
Oh how I would like to be on your big back.

Lust and love

Lust will die but love never did,
When you love someone,
It is forever,
When you lust after another,
Love is absent,
Soon lust will turn to hate,
Love is felt without the present,
The soul is love,
And it can never be possessed,
Love is of the spirit,
That dwells in the soul,
Within the body.

Allah is the Greatest

Man thinks that he can penetrate the heavens as he wish,
But only by the leave of Allah does he get beyond Earth,
There is only one who can create life and rule the Earth,
And all that is out in the universe,
Allah is the greatest,
No man knows anything when he is in the womb,
Allah is the creator of all knowledge and he gave man the sciences,
There is no one who knows what tomorrow will bring,
Though man plans, Allah plans too,
And he only can see and hear all that is in the Earth and in
paradise,
Allah is the greatest,
No man can bring one thing into existence.
Without Allah approval–

Steve Biko

Must freedom have so high a price,
Lives stole by the oppressor for fun,
Black consciousness is smothered with your breath,
But the youth will carry out your dream,
Black is supreme and will rise again,
The king of Nubia will rise again,
Strong black men would rule,
The spirit of Chaka you did stand for,
Bring on the destroyer,
We will win in the end.

Revolution Now

Liberation is something that happens to the soul,
Rebellion is the beginning of struggle,
Until you have a real program, a real ideology,
you rebel against oppression,
When you have rationalized that the only thing you want,
is complete autonomy from the oppressor,
And you are willing to lay down your life,
so that your children will have a future free of oppression,
Then you are ready for revolution.

Huey Newton

The supreme servant of the people,
Who gunned you down,
Was it the dope dealers who hated mada,
Was it the pigs who you hated more,
Could the aggrevashious _________ men paid for it
Who paid your killer,
What

The supreme servant of the people,
You gave your life for the people,
When you stood up to
Those who oppress the Black people,
Your courage was your weapon,
You live in the youth of today,
Struggling to create
A just society for all

I Moved Today

I moved out of home base today,
I am determined this time l will stay,
Allah is on my side and to him I do pray,
I will let him guide me this time forever,
I will stay on the best side of him,
I will doubt my lord no more,
I know I have a special destiny,
I stay prepared because one never knows when he might go,
I will hold onto his mercy,
For surely he has blessed me this day.

Holy Than Thou

Some black women think they can fool Allah,
But Allah is aware of all their plans,
They destroy the faith of their men,
Doubting the man's judgement,
They profess to be so holy and filled with spirit,
That their human needs are suppress for a while,
Yet they emerge as all nature must be fulfilled,
These women live in lie
They follow the supernatural belief in celebrities,
But their bodies are not super natural,
And must be fulfilled.

Black life

Why is it always the black one,
When the destroyer comes he looks to kill the black one,
The destroyer knows it is the black one,
That will destroy him,
The black one possess the melanin and is a threat to his whiteness,
His blackness will destroy the light one,
The cold has destroyed the heat of love,
Conditions has created the destroyer,
Never will he live in peace,
He is greedy and envious of your rod,
He hates his skin because it is disappeared,
Only you can take away the fearful.
But that black one when it reproduces,
Will bring more of the melanin,
That will mean the annihilation of the weak, white, germ,
That is destined to die out,
The end will come and all that will be left,
Is the black world.

Brown Eyed Girl

Beautiful brown eyed girl,
From you came the perfect world,
The world of Egypt and Kush
You gave the world its first civilization,
When you laugh I see the world anew,
When you cry I see rain in the forest,
There is no beginning or end to you.
Before you there was none,
And after you their will be no more,
Beautiful brown eyed girl,
You are a cultured pearl,
Before you will come the whole world,
To bow in your present,
And say you are the black Pharaoh Queen.

Tripping

Throbbing water holes come to the surface of my mind,
Overflowing streams rush my heart,
Lost worlds appear at my eyes,
New creatures come forward,
Time ceases to move, space and sound stand still,
Vagueness grasps my unconscious thoughts,
I hear sounds far away,
I see new colors,
Many nights turn into future days,
I feel exhausted or inspired to write.

I Need Time Off

I need time off to be in the company of my lover,
When I look into her hazel eyes I see the years flow,
I see the beaches and the sea,
I need time off to run free in the park where Indian caves hide you from the crowd,
I need time off to barbeque steaks and hamburgers on the camp ground grill,
I need time off to sit in a Persian restaurant where there are fine wines, and a mystic scenery,
I need time off to travel to Crator lake and look upon the clear water surrounded by snow,
I need time off to frolic along the beaches of big sun
I need time off to ride the rides at play land,
I need time off to visit the lake in Tahoe to sit with a fluttering butterfly,
To ride the train up into the mountainside,
I need time off to live again.

Steve Biko

Must freedom have so high a price,
Lives stolen by the oppressor for fun,
Black consciousness is smothered with your breath,
But the youth will carry out your dream,
Black is supreme and will rise again,
The kings of Nubia will rise again,
Strong black men who would rule,
The spirit of Chaka you did stand for,
Just as he was betrayed by his own,
so were you.

Black Mother

Thou they strip you of power,
You did survive by a new invention,
You acquiesce to overcome your trials,
Yet today it is a man that will make you a woman,
Without a man a woman is nothing but a WOE?
THE BLACK MAN HAS RISEN!

Free Mandela Now

We won't wait on the old world to give him to us,
We will fight and make it so,
Stop looking for sympathy from the destroyer,
He has no interest in your tears,
It only makes him more cruel,
Lets breakdown the system,
Let us destroy our enemy,
Bring him home to a free people,
Willing to die for independence.

Hostages

We are hostages in the enemies camp,
Held for ransom by being the mans ticket for progress on a human level,
Lost in the mans world of gadgets and security qualifications,
Black hostages of the USA,
Loan to a foreign government to fight a foolish war,
Bought by wall street to show progress and is window dressing,
Proof of our progress is shown by a few successes,
Time is our friend, because it never stop changing, giving us proof of our captivity.

Goodbye Love

You made me so happy,
Why did you give up on love,
Goodbye love,
Yes when I walked at night it seems that God love our might,
Goodbye love,
Upon the alter of love I cast my pearls,
Goodbye love,
In the garden of paradise I wanted you to be my wife,
Goodbye love,
The shores of the mighty seas,
Brought your love to me in times of need,
Goodbye love,
Music oh sweet music gave our love the love songs of our time,
Goodbye love.

Mother Nature

I got love for you
Darling my love for you runs deep,
Deep as the sea and it roars like the waves,
It tells the world how I love thee,
Sweet in the night we met,
Sweet was the love we made,
I got love for you,
When I hold your tender hands I can't resist,
My love for you can take me to bliss,
I got love for you.

Look Not Upon The Face Of Death,

Look not back or you will be turn to salt,
Live only with your own,
Don't try to live with the enemy,
He will burn the cross,
He will hate you,
Because you are beauty,
Look upon my face it is Africa,
It is the face of God,
What! You do not believe,
Go to the pyramids,
They are permanent and if you see a black African,
You see the God,
Amen,
Reach for the sun,
And it will come to you,
All the work is God.

Loneliness

I have known lonely days,
Where there is no music,
Days that seem to linger and whine,
I have known hours to pass with the day,
Hours filled with nothing but silence,
I have known nights that are bare,
Nights without any tenderness or love,
Midnights that come without the joy of another day,
I have known loneliness.

Smile on you

When I see your eyes I smile on you,
Beholding your hips my soul smiles on you
The thought of your broad hips,
I smile on you,
Your nappy hair is mystical,
I smile on you
The shine of your golden black skin,
God smiles on you,
His first creation,
Bares the soul of the beginning of man.

Solidarity With The People Of South Africa

We are one,
You in South Africa,
And us of the world,
Your chains are a part of us,
Where there is one African in bondage,
The whole race is in chains,
Your freedom shall be our freedom,
When you utter Uhurce we say freedom

Panama

Here lies the truth made plain violence is a tool reserved only for
the capitalist,
When anyone else uses violence against the capitalist he is a
terrorist,
America is so self-righteous that she even sees her evil as a virtue,
She is the arrogant whore that she commits numerous crimes in the
name of Democracy,
The treaty with Panama doesn't give America the right to
dictate to their government,
If Norega is a criminal then Bush is his partner in crime,
We hold America responsible for the Vietnam war crimes,
We hold her responsible for the Congo, El Salvadore, Bolivia
Nigeria, Palestine,
America makes dictators so that she can invade others land for
their resources.

Africa for the Africans

Africans are in rebellion against neo-colonialism and the
nations must come through struggle. The struggle that
the masses wage to put away foreign domination and the
reinstatement of their cultural life.
Europe is control and exploited by the European,
Asia is own and exploited by the Asians,
Africa is not own and exploited for the benefit of the African,
Therefore, we say that there will be no peace until the
Land of our ancestors are free.
Africa for the Africans at home and around world.

Highway 49

I left my good home behind,
I am traveling down highway 49,
I can see no light,
I should have waited for the sunrise,
Because its all black at night,
Down here on highway 49,
I am only going further down south,
Where knowledge is no good,
Only your colors can make you sow,
Down here on highway 49.

Frozen in Time

I have seen minutes that were eternal,
Each minute of life in a search to be joined with the divine,
What has the modern man forgotten
That life was perfect,
That the being that one destroys is not their creation,
Man must commune with nature,
Modern man pursuit of wealth to the extreme,
That they will kill millions with their greed,
Oh man how has the native world delude thee.
The land is God's
The sky he created
So you would have space
Earth is your home

Who Am I

Could man change what God created within,
What have I done with what the creator gave me,
I know that I have not realized my potential,
Must I go to him and ask for guidance,
What if he has given up on me,
The one being that cannot give up is my lord,
He waits on me with eternal patience,
I must go out and conquer,
This, the spirit of the Divine has set within my being
That I must control the life I live
The one that can produce my joy
Only you can create your happiness.

Black First

We should love us first,
That is black folk should love self first,
We should help self first,
The fact is we don't support our own,
Our jazz musicians must play in some white joint to make it,
The fact is our musicians must please the other culture,
When they are considered as making it,
Our writers rely on the majority other to be published,
The fact is we all must be used by others to earn a living,
We must be for our self.
Throw off dependence
And make our way together.

The black man's god and creator,
When Ptah conceived in his heart mankind,
And created from the earth man,
And gave him the image of himself,
The loving spirit of God cause man to be a living creature,
When Osiris the first of the ancestors,
Created the offspring
Of his kind by His mate, Isis
Heru, the son of the living God.
By the Immaculate Conception.

Religious Uncle Toms

These are the black liberals,
Who the oppressor uses to keep you positive,
He knows that you will identify with your own,
The religious uncle toms are our novacaine,
When you see what is happening to us,
They use these black liberals,
Who tell you its your fault,
This is a good country,
You can make it,
Yet he lives off your oppressor.

Days of Resistance

When the child has come of age,
When he sees the difference in our lives,
Where white people are in a paradise,
And our family is on an assistance,
Not much for the they insist,
We the people of color can clearly see,
What has been stolen from us,
The land makes one rich and successful,
Our success is our land.

Your own choice

You love me by your own choice,
I love you because my heart choice,
I try to live my life so we could last forever,
You say your love is real and will be always,
I love because all my life I have waited,
You seem to never let go,
When we love it seems as if the world is better
You never ask me to show,
That's why the love we have was never before created.

Death is a Drummer

Death is a drummer,
Beating until the last ant goes into its hole,
Until the last dew drop falls,
Death is a drummer,
Beating until the last eye is closed,
Until man draws its last breath,
Death is a drummer,
Beating until the last word is uttered,
Until nothing remains,
But Olodumare.is left to create a new world.

Death is a song

Death is a song,
Singing until the last melody is sung,
Singing until the sun rises no more,
Until there is no moon,
Death is a song,
Singing until the last mouth uttered a word,
Until the rhythm stops and the music ends,
Death is a song,
Until the last singer has sang,
Death is a song, until Olodumare comes.

Awake the Black Race

How long must we wait to be avenged,
Vengeance is with the Lord,
We forgive yet they keep on murdering us,
We love and they keep on torturing us,
They make us drink boiling water,
When will the black man stop loving his natural enemy,
Wake up black man,
Stand up and fend yourself,
Self-preservation is the first law.

The Colfax Massacre

Woe to the murder
Woe to killers, God will have no mercy,
God will have no mercy,
How long oh Lord,
Will they kill the innocent,
Yesterday it was the Colfax 150,
They dug a big pit,
And killed 150 Black people,
They kill us because we are black, a color,
We were the ones who strove to vote,
Today its Sharpeville and Soweto

Somalia

What, America is doing something for the black man,
I wonder what the hidden motive is,
Profit or some angle,
What about the black people here that need,
What about South Africa,
Can America overlook the flagrant violations of apartheid,
Where Africans are not allowed to look for work,
Where children are killed like dogs,
What about Soweto.

You Are Good For Me

You wake me up to a good hot breakfast,
Baby you are right on time,
Then you make sweet love to me,
Baby then you get my bath water ready,
You have my clothes cleaned and ironed,
Then you kiss me goodbye,
That is when I leave to go to work,
But you have to work so we can meet our bills,
You call me on your lunch break to tell me you miss me so,
our love bed a manger,
Our song was "Always",
Yet today it is goodbye and we don't make love no ways,
Upon the alter of love and romance,
We danced to a thousand songs,
Our love dance was close to each other,
Yet today we are far apart from one another.

What is Life When You Control Nothing

You are a feather in the wind,
We have been moved about too long,
Let us take control of our destiny,
Lets move on our own,
Don't be a pawn in the name of life,
Move over to the side of people who are free,
Let us decide where we want to be,
Let us decide how we look,
Let us build cities and nations.
In the image of Kemil, our holy land (Egypt)

Wild and sweet

I am looking for a love wild and sweet,
One love that can make me see,
How she loves me as a lollipop,
One love that makes my heart surrender,
A love that can take me in the night,
Our love will be one that all will remember,
A love that is clearly out of sight,
A love that can feel that's life for real...

Happy Life

Cheerful joy is the peoples hate,
The people are hateful to people who love,
If you get more than them they hate you fiercely,
They are like crabs in a can,
They don't let anyone out of their circle of poverty,
Why don't we love each other's success,
All we want is to party until we sweat,
And don't let no one get more that then rest,
Poverty call us all to become a mess.

Church

Black folks assemble in their tribes,
Gleam and love in their eyes,
Love is streaming I the air,
Children sing sweet hymns and cry,
Old women jump and shout,
Preachers spread the word about,
God's mercy descends as we come to make amends.

Why El Salvador

Reagan demands a change with the gun,
Yet tells us we should not take our independence with a sword or violence,
How can we upset the hold that poverty has on us,
What must be done,
Awaken the workers of America as the rich plays on the world the old trick.
Let the poor have hope of being rich,
While America fight the poor warrior with canons,
And some people wait only for the mailman.

Atomic Woman

From the very atom of your life,
I see you dancing like a playful bird,
Upon the disco floor,
Atomic Woman,
I see you over a hot stove cooking for others,
Atomic Woman,
Oh how safe is the ride when she drives the bus,
How beautiful is the love you make in the night,
Atomic Woman,
Feed your child the knowledge we lost across the sea.
The children are the future, teach them well.

The God of America

What! You have a contract with Allah,
That said when ever you kill, steal, murder,
That you are forgiven by Jesus who paid for your sin,
It's a dangerous world where mankind is not responsible for their actions,
Thus you create a society that will sanction murder,
That to kill a non-white person is not a crime,
Miami one dead while on a motorcycle,
Baton rouge another dead while approaching a house with a killer inside.
Wars for to steal the gifts God gave mankind
God never gave you the U.S.A

The Black Untouchables

The black underclass is the new untouchables,
The black middle class identifies with the European values and concepts,
Through their education they puss out of the race,
Onto the "main stream",
They live close to the European rulers of a stolen land,
They reap the benefit of siding with the ruling Caucasians,
Their behavior among the untouchables,
Are the reflection of their fiend arrogant America,
They even spout the same party lines of their friends,
Build more jails,
They are nothing but criminals, and their favorite shows are police stories,
They are not in touch with the oppression of the brothers,
They say as their bosses,
Pull yourself up by your boot straps as I did.
Yet they forget that the underclass has no boots,
Come home brothers and lets build a stronger bond than materialism, the enemy of Africans.

The Myth Of Black Capitalism

The enemy makes it sounds as if he worked to be rich,
Three hundred years of free labor made it that way,
Capitalism needs someone to exploit,
It is based on the based on the idea of man exploiting another man,
Black capitalism in a facade for the manipulation of the middle class,
They believe that the capitalist in America,
Worked hard to be rich,
They used the raw material of the third world to feed their factories,
The labor of the worker is used to finish the product from their raw materials,
Blacks lack access to the resources to field a capitalist of economy.

Panama

Here lies the truth made plain, volence is a tool reserved only for the capitalist,
When anyone else uses violence against the capitalist he is a terrorist,
America is so self-righteous that she even sees her evil as a virtue,
She is the arrogant whore that commits numerous crimes in the name of democracy,
If Noreega is a criminal then Bush is his partner in crime,
We hold America responsible for the war crimes,
We hold her responsible for the Congo, El Salvador, Bolivia,
America makes dictators so that she can invade others land for their resources.

Coletrain the liberator

A love supreme, a love supreme,
The creator loves all creation,
He never look on anyone man with special favors,
It is up to the black man to free himself
The notions of inferiority is propagated by a white society,
We must take our Afrocentricity to its logical end,
Culturally Coletrain amplifies what must be done,
He took jazz as played from a revolutionary vision,
And stamped upon the blackmind,
A new level of consciousness.

Addicted

When a man craves something,
He looses control of his body,
He loses control of his mind,
His mind is rampant and his will is cripple,
He becomes helpless before the world,
So many times he loses that which he love,
A woman, a friend, a family,
And sometimes he loses his very life,
He is the poorest of the poor.

When I Was Young

When I was young they would hurt me with white hate,
Then I would turn on myself,
I would become enraged and eat dirt and chew grass,
They would say your black skin ugly,
I would become angry and fight,
But my consoler would also say you are ugly,
And they all would laugh,
My God, My God,
Jehovah would laugh and side with my haters,
Later on I found Allah the god of the mixed,
And he would tell me you are black and beautiful,
And I would look at the leaders and they were mixed,
I would look at what was propagated and who would be favored and they were mixed,
I listen to the word and it said,
The light penetrated the darkness,
The darkness was upon the face of the Earth,
Then there was light

Black life

Where in the black life,
Has it died before its birth,
When will it appear in the black,
Allah is the first and last supreme black,
Knowledge precedes from his clear blackmind,
Clear the mind of man to understanding,
Black life,
The movement of the black world,
Which carry the seed of new life,
Why has the black woman choose other than the dark man,
She now prefers others who will lighten her child,
Lord, Lord, has the black man failed in this life?
Or is it a trick?
To divide the Race

The First Time

When we were innocents
And our love was pure
Then we fell in love,
Your eyes shine with joy,
Your body was moved to ecstasy,
Deep inside I felt a river of love flowing,
Yet we had not made life,
All together we strove for the source of love,
The night stood still as we embraced,
And rain beat on the window seals.
The first time

How can America survive when she refuses to acknowledge known criminals,
Criminals with a badge who were caught on national t.v.
And yet the brutes all freed by white justice,
Has anything changed since slavery,
When blacks had no rights the white man respected,
Are we still chatted or citizens of the U.S.A.
Stand up, stand up
We must make our retribution our goal.

Another beaten nearly to death,
And an all white fury sets the perpetrator free,
Its because to kill is to kill a white person here,
If you kill a non-white person you are justified,
Murder a whole nation and steal their property,
This isn't a crime but a nations manifest destiny.

Living Like A Leaf

Bold you must be or you live like a leaf,
Going wherever the wind blow,
There are no roots to sow,
Over the land you fly
As a leaf I float through the sky,
You never come down
Until the wind stop and you hit the ground,
Each day goes by in a flutter,
And life bring you to the gutter, I
Joy is a lost hope then some turned to dope,
Empty is your heart,
Sadness seem to never part,
Your thoughts fly away like a butterfly,
And you lose the will to try,
Only the strong survive,
Be keen and you will stay alive,
What purpose is the pain,
While all day dreams never seem to remain,
Living like a leaf,
When life is so brief.

I Beg Your Pardon

What! Did you see the front page of Newsweek,
Is this America,
Mass hysterical in the press,
Iraq is angry at the U.S.
But what have we done to them,
What can cause us to hate,
Is the zeal for God to hate what he created,
This really is,
The hate that hate created,
How can we now hate what we so willing encourage,
We were cheering when Iraq was being invaded,
We stood by while innocent people were slaughtered.
Why! Did we watch people die from chemical warfare,
We tallied with the wild dog when it attacked those Arabs we hate,
Yet when our oil supplies are threatened we paint Hussein as a
mad dog,
Human life is expandable but oil is not,
We knew that he would kill,
Just as with Hitler.
America why don't you see the hand writing on the wall,
South Africa invaded Nabia or Namblia,
We only sigh,
America! Has it only interest become material wealth?
National interest is only oil or wealth,
People die we only sigh.

The God in Me

I know the god in me
You must conquer the satan in me,
I stood naked to the world
But the satan preferred,
It with clothes on,
What is it that the devil has done,
And where is his hiding place,
They say he had the key
But Jerus descend to Hell,
And took the keys to Hell,
What are the keys to Heaven,
They are with him.
The God of gods.

Me

I am the beginning of me,
I am the end of me,
I am motion, forever becoming,
Perpetua I motion,
I am because we are,
Therefore we are,
Because I am,
I am that lam the boundless,
The infinite,
I am because he lives in me,
From the beginning I am that I am was here until the end of time.

Madness blues

Hated by the owners of this land,
Scorned by the women in their hand,
My color is held as my shame,
No one really knows my name,
My manhood taken by both man and woman,
I fight with the words but no one hears my cries,
This voice in the wilderness of an arrogant land,
May the false gods go cause they are on the side of madness,
I wait because maybe they are drunk with power or badness,
Over and above the cause of truth,
I look back and see where the burdens of youth,
Yet I still hear the phone ring,
I still feel the sting of my denial of self.

Right Skin

We are held in check,
Because our skin is black,
They think they own the world,
Because their skin is white,
Their superiority is based on our inferiority,
Where are the black man's religions,
We all are under the dooms day belief,
Christianity with its hereafter,
Which has made us slaves
And then masters.

Hanibal

Oh where has he gone,
We need him today,
Yesterday he led us through mountains with elephants,
We conquer the enemy with his skill leading us,
Forsake Jesus,
He led us to death,
We need our own.
It is not our nature to be meek and submissive to evil,
Our legacy is one of warriors that protects his life.

Late Night

In our community the police are here to oppress,
In the other community they are there to protect,
When we need a policeman he only comes to arrest,
What crimes has this nigger community done tonight,
There are no citizens only criminals,
When you see more than two of them together you know its trouble,
The other community gets drunk and crowd the street,
But they are only teenagers trying to have fun,
But those niggers are up to something with their gang,
When you see these black teenagers he is only a face,
If the niggers get rowdy in their community we must bust some heads.

E T Cafe

There is a place in this town,
Where the drunkards and the dope fiend is renown, E T Cafe,
Where they share a bottle of Tokay,
Here the crack men get rich,
And here the dope fiend loses his mind in smoke,
And sober people are the joke,
Here the cocaine is turned into coke,
Music is about the blues,
When they get home the key jump back in their hand,
He left home a man,
But when he returned from the E T Cafe,
He is only a thang.

Baby Come Back

Oh baby come back,
To a love,n”,’. .tronO6Q
A love that will do you.@ wrong.
onlb”by come back,
To be with you takes me to a higher plane,
Without you life wont be the same,
Oh baby come back,
Why do we go from heaven to hell,
We really have done well,
Oh baby come back,
Don’t leave me here in love wonderland,
., !t/
You ma{qre feel like a natural man.

Baby Come Over

Girl what are you doing today,
Why don't you come over to play,
Let us lay and listen to the lightning,
As we lay in a quiet storm booming,
Baby come over,
Let us make time and fall in love,
As the gods fight in the heavens above,
Baby come over,
Let us dance to love songs,
Let our love grow strong.

Breakfast

Suppose we were food,
And every morning the biscuit would bite us,
Then the bacon would be us
The grits would swallow us slowly,
Mixed with saliva we would slide gently to our end,
And the milk would consume us in one gulp,
The eggs would devour us as it reads the morning paper,
The orange juice would only want a taste of us,
If we were food,
There would be few people,
Getting up early so that they could be eaten by food today.

Black Hope

One day we will be one,
The black man will be a unit of one,
The black woman will love and respect us,
We will protect her in our unity,
Every black person will be free,
No more slaves will we be,
The rules of the world will be our own,
The black men will all be home, t
Africa, Africa
You will rise
To put down the suppressing tide.

Patrice

We will not be your monkey no more,
We will not be your victim no longer,
Africa, Africa
We will not live by your laws no more,
I won't be your monkey no more,
I will not be your victim no longer,
Give me Uhuru,
I am with the mau mau,
I destroy all obstacles in my path.

Malcom X to me

When my friend gave me a copy of the autobiography of
Malcom x,
I read it from cover to cover without stopping even for a cigarette,
I became a new man that no longer believes in non-violence,
I wanted to know more about the prophet that changed black
America,
I read the books that had influenced him,
I wanted to understand the movement he was in,
I read Elijah Muhammad's book,
Messate to the black man,
I wanted to better understand what had changed him,
I knew from the moment I put his book down,
I was now what we students called a "Malcomite",
I had visions of a new black man that loved his Afrocentricity,
I was now proud of my African Ancestry,
It would take a while for me to see that the black woman,
was my natural mate,
That I would hate the evils repeated against,
My African brother,
I listen to his tapes and fell in love with his militancy,
I would quote him constantly every day,
I laugh at his humor,
And rave at his anger,
I saw in me a new man,
That wanted freedom for black people, by any means necessary.

Human Rights

What are our basis rights as human beings,
We are entitled to the rights to life, liberty and the pursuit of
happiness,
We are entitled to be treated as human beings with feelings
that are affected by other human actions,
We are entitled to jobs that enable us to live like descent people,
We are entitled to land to live on,
We are entitled to the rights accorded by the U.S. constitution,
Our labor should be for the benefit of our own.

White Justice

What! The mad dogs are loose again,
Policeman dealing out the brutality of the people,
People who have no regard for black life,
Rodney King is in a long line of martyr blacks,
What happened in LA was not an actual accident,
This is the mentality of an oppressor,
What crime had our ancestors done,
When they were captured and tortured by the enslaver
What crimes had those 100,000,000 black Africans had
committed,
The imperialist knows no rights of the oppress,
When we know that the policemen are backed by the judges.

Allah Wills

Let mankind give thanks because all things come from him,
Our good times are a hindrance to sublime feelings of beings in accord with the will of Allah,
Of a fly was to snatch away something from man,
He is helpless,
Can man create a fly,
Only God is the creator of life,
Allah is the greatest,
Who so ever compete with him will be thrown,
Into Hell fire,
Glory is his cloak,
And majesty is his crown.

The liberals

They are the novocain,
They make you think that what happened to you is your fault,
When you rise up to kill the oppressor,
He push a liberal upfront,
The liberal tells you go slow,
All of us are not like that,
I am your friend,
I don't want to kill the innocent,
Yet we live our lives off your oppression.

Plow the Earth

When fore fathers bent over a plow,
We were the twinkle in his eye,
The sweat in his brow,
You would be our tear,
Today we are not free,
Because thou you plow the Earth,
We are not apart of the fund,
Only Amen Ra can make you free,
Free the land.

Lust and Love!

Lust will Die,
But Love never Did,
When you Love someone, It is forever,
When you Lust after Another. Love is Absent,
Soon Lust will turn to Hate,
Love is felt without the present.
The Soul is Love,
And it can never be Possessed
Love is of the Spirit.
That Dwells in the Soul within the Body!

Words of Castles

Build Black man,
Take your Life from is et,
The evil of the bottle,
The evil of the pipe,
From the evil of the needle,
Rise up black man,
From the stale breath of crack
From the sleep of Heroine
From the estacy of cocaine,
Build lives of goodness,
And sacrifice for the love of the children,
Rise up Black man,
From self hate that deny your own responsibility,
Rise up from unproductive lives,
Build castles of Golden ones
Build your world of wonders.

I Smile on You

When I see your beautiful black eyes,
I smile on you
Beholding your hips,
My soul smile on you,
The thoughts of your broad hips,
I smile on you
Your nappy hair is mythical
I smile on you
The shine of your Golden Black skin,
God smiles on you,
His first creation of you
The sun shines on you,
Bares the soul of the
Beginning of humankind.

Look not upon the face of Death

Look not before you will be turned to salt
Live only with your own
Don't try to live with the enemy
He will burn the cross,
He will hate you
Because you are Beauty,
Look upon my face it is afraid
It is the face of God,
What! You do not believe,
Go to the pyramids,
Look upon the face of the sphinx
And it you see a Blue African
You'll see the God Amen Ra,
See the face of God Amen Ra in Egypt land.

You are Good for me

You wake me up to a good hot breakfast,
Baby you are right on time,
Then you make sweet love to me,
Baby then u get my bath water ready,
You have my clothes clean and iron,
Then you kiss me goodbye
That is when I leave to go to work.
But you have to work so we can meet our bills,
You call me on your lunch break to tell me you miss me so
Our love bed a manger,
Our song was "Always"
Yet today it is goodbye and we don't make love no ways
Upon the altar of love and romance
We danced to a thousands songs,
Our love dance was close to each other,
Yet today we are apart from one another.

What is life when you control nothing?

You are only a feather in the wind,
We have been move about too long,
Let us take control of our destiny,
Lets move on our own,
Don't be a pawn in the name of life,
Move over to the side of people who are free,
Let us decide where we want to be,
Let us decide how we look,
Let us build cities and nations.

Wild and Sweet

I am looking for a love wild and sweet,
One love that can make me see
How she love me as a lollipop,
One love that make my heart surrender,
A love that can take me in the night,
Our love will be one that all will remember,
A love that is clearly out of sight,
A love that can feel that's life for real..

Happy Life

Cheerful Joy is the peoples hate,
The people are hateful to people who love,
If you get more than them they hate you fiercely,
They are like crabs in a can,
They don't let anyone out of their circle of poverty,
Why don't we love each others success,
All we want is to party until we sweat,
And don't let no one get more that the rest,
Poverty call us all to become a mess.

Church

Black folks assemble in their tribes
Gleam and love in their eyes
Love streaming in the air
Children sing sweet hymns and cry
Old women jump and shout
Preachers spread the word about
God's mercy decends as we come to make amends.

Why El Salvadofe?

Reagan demands a change with the gun,
Yet tells us we should not take our independence with a sword or violence.
How can we upset the hold that poverty has on us?
What must be done?
Awaken workers of America as the rich plays on the world the old trick.
Let the poor have hope of being rich.
While America fight the poor warrior with canons,
And the people wait only for the mailman.

Atomic Woman

From the very atom of your life,
I see you Dancing like a playful bird,
Upon the disco floor,
Atomic Woman,
I see you over a hot stove cooking for others,
Atomic Woman
I see you sitting on a stool pushing so others may ride,
Atomic Woman
Oh how safe is the ride when she drive the bus,
How beautiful is the love you make in the night
Atomic Woman
Feed your child the knowledge we lost across sea.

I need time off

I need time off to be in the company of my lover,
When I look into her hazel eyes I see the years flow,
I see the beaches and the sea
I need time off to run free in the park where Indian
caves hides you from the crowd,
I need time off to sit in a Persian restaurant where there
are fine wines, and mystic scenery.
I need time off to travel to crator lake and look upon
the clear water surrounded by snow,
I need time off to frolic along the beaches of big sur,
I need time off to ride the rides at play land,
I need time off to visit the lake in tahoe to sit with
a fluttering butterfly,
To ride the train up into the mountainside
I need time off to live again.

Tripping

Throbbing water holes come to the surface of my mind.
Overflowing streams rush my heart.
Lost worlds appear at my eyes.
New creatures come forward,
Many nights turn to future days.
Time ceases to move, space and sound stand still.
Vagueness grasps my unconscious thoughts.
I hear sounds far away
I see new colors
I feel exhausted or inspired to write.

Steve Biko

Must freedom have so high aprice,
Lives stilen by the oppressor for fun
Black consciousness is smothered with your breath.
But the youth will carry out your dream black
Black is supreme and will rise again
The kings of Nubia will rise again
Strong black men who would rule
The spirit of Chaka you did stand for
Just as he was betrayed by his own son was you

Black Mother!

thou they strip you of Power,
you did survive by a New Invention,
You acquice to over come your trials,
Yet today it is a man, that will make you a new Woman.
without a man a woman is nothing but WOE?
THE BLACK MAN HAS RISEN!

Free Mandela Now

We won't wait on the old world to give him to us,
We will fight and make it so,
Stop looking for sympathy from the destroyer,
He has no interest in your tears,
It only make him more cruel,
Lets breakdown the system,
Let us destroy our enemy
Bring his home to a free people
Willing to die for independence.

Hostages

We are hostages in the enemies camp,
Held for ransom by being the man's
ticket for progress on a human level,
Lost in the man's world of gudgets and
security qualifications,
Black hostages of the USA
Loan to Foreign government to
Fight a foolish war,
Bought by wall street to show progress
and is window dressing,
Proof of our progress is shown by
a few successes
Time is our friend, because it never
stop changing, giving us proof of
our captivity.

Goodbye Love

You made me so happy.
Why did you give up on love,
Goodbye love,
Yes when I walked at night it seems that Good love our might,
Good love,
Upon the altar of love I cast my pearls,
Good love,
In the garden of paradise I wanted you to be my wife,
Good love,
The shores of the mighty seas,
Brought your lobe to me in times of need,
Good love,
Music, oh sweet music our love the love songs of our time,
Good love.

I Got Love for you

Darling my love for you run
Deep like the sea,
My love is a roaring see and
they roll up the waves of the sea,
It tells the world how I love thee,
Sweet is the night we met,
Sweet is the love we made
I got love for you,
When I hold your tenderness,
I just can't resist,
My love for you takes me to bliss,
I got love for you,
This feeling keep on,
Forever my love exist.

Loneliness

I have known lonely days
Where there is no music
Days that seem to linger and whine
I have known hours that last
It seem for days,
Hours filled with nothing but silence,
I have known night that are bare of dreams,
Midnights that come with out
joy of another day,
I have known loneliness,
Bare with ghosts of terror,
From thought of forever in a minute,
From thoughts of forever,
Without another day,
Alone, drifting, still and not moving.

Bud

Buddy monk comes to mind,
Old but yet in his youth,
As a man everlasting,
He is the man for all seasons,
He comes to me at the river bank,
With flocals and artifacts,
Of our life here in the USA,
Bud I can always count on you,
You are sunshine on a rainy day.

I promise myself

Never to worry again,
Because worry never did nothing
But think of what not to do
Never to do wat you need to do,
I tried to do what I need to do,
But worry only let me think of
what I did not do,
Never what I need to do or
What needs to be done,
I need to be doing what
need to be done,
I promise to do what I
Need to do myself.
I need to do it right.
I need to take my time and
do it right,
I need to take my time and
do it right,
And do it tonight.
Take the time,
Take my time and do it right.
Even if it takes all night
I need to do it right
I know I can do it right
Even if it takes all night.

Elaine—the Soothe sayer—

She said I was born 50 years ahead of my time
That means I am 41 years old instead of 71 years old.
This is my cosmic age
The universe brought me forth
30 years ahead of my time,
The universe brought ahead of time
Me to let me know I was to be
her son and her lover
Black Queen Nefertari you are a Queen,
Supreme,
Your majestic aura inspires
me to be your King
Time will one day declare our love
Truth cast me in Kemil where
you were with me,
Today is Tomorrow and yesterday is Today-
Oh Queen of Queen you are
What time has ordained for me

Memoirs of Carrie Lee Davis and her Impact on my Life

My Mother's Life and My Family's Background

Carrie L. Davis, my mother was born February 3, 1920. Her maiden name was Carrie Lee Helaire. She was a sharecropper in her middle years. Moreover, she was a maid to a family of whites at the age of 9. Her mother's name was Emily Hamilton. Her father's name was Benjamin Helaire. He was soft spoken and quiet, but firm in ways on raising children. However, he had an impact one way our mother raised her eight children.

Over the years, she would often make the comment that her father and her mother would often say that a parent could always discipline their children even after they were grown. Thus, she would often say that her father was strict and very mean. In my interview with her in March 2001, she stated that her father taught her to be firm and strict on her children.

My mother had a 7th grade education, however years later when she was in her forties she obtained her high school diploma. For, initially, when she was much younger she dropped out of school to help work on her father's farm.

Throughout her life, my mother taught her children from the bible through words and pictures. Thus, my mother was an avid reader. However, she read any and everything she could find. Throughout her life, she would study with people who were missionaries in the community. Thus, my mother taught us to respect nature and to observe the animals and plant-life around us. For, she would always tell us to observe the animals and how they bent their knee to reverence God before they would sleep. Thus, she said that the trees would bend to the wind and praise the lord who made them. Furthermore, she taught us to pray before sleeping and to pray the first thing in the morning. Hence, when it was raining she taught us to pray while God was doing his work.

In life, my mother was blessed with eight children. As a result of her commitment to education, she was able to raise eight children, all of which obtained a college education. Thus, she was persistent to see that we all got the best education we could. For, my mother encouraged all the children she would meet to go to college and finish their education to be prepared for life. Thus, I believe her upbringing had a lot to do with her views toward education and uplift.

My mother grew up in Bermuda, Louisiana. This was a rural community south of Natchitoches, Louisiana. There were numerous plantations and farms in this area. My mother grew up on the Oakland plantation, which has become a national historic site. Oakland plantation was home to eight African American families. In recent years, I have visited the site and notice that the houses that the families lived in are still standing. For, my mother told me, that when she was growing up the people would assemble under a big pecan tree in the middle of the community. This was an African American tradition that was passed down from generation to generation.

Later, in my interview, my mother described to me how her father made a living. She told me that he was a butcher and a dock worker as well as a sharecropper. Furthermore, she said that the men often worked in the winter and in the fall at other jobs while the rest of the family worked in the fields. Thus, she explained how her father was considered a rebel in the eyes of the plantation owners, for he bootlegged whiskey. She also mentions her grandfather, John Helaire, who worked for Frenchmen in the area. Thus, he inherited their French name. Thus, her grandfather was a slave until he was ten years old. My mother mentions the African all the time. Furthermore, she would always mention how her grandfather was always running away from the plantation when he was a young man.

My mother worked from the time she was seven years old. For, she kept the children for the Prudhomme family at Oakland plantation. As a result, she was taken on trips to different places by the family. Over the years she worked at the plantation, she went to Chicago, New York and St. Louis, Missouri. During this time, my mother was given 50 cents a week. Furthermore, my mother worked in the fields, for her parents were sharecroppers. It is important to note that this was the period in black history where black people were re-enslaved to the landowners. Thus, the themselves. At this time, labor is now dominated by capital. For after the Civil War, Blacks had smashed the chattel slavery. Hence workloads were separated by seasons due to anticipated profits for only the landowners.

Thus, in the summer, my mother would work the meat on the farm and smoke it for the winter. Thus, she stated that she would work the whole year and would not make any money off of the cotton crop. Hence, my mother worked in sugar cane fields. It was the hardest job she ever worked. As a result of harvesting the sugar cane, they were forced to make syrup and sugar from the cane for the winter. Thus, she stated that her whole family worked in the fields, for it did not matter how small you were. The conditions of seasonal work was so demanding, for, they were asked to travel and cultivate many crops that her family once moved to Alexandria for a year.

Later in an interview with my mother, she explained to me that her grandfather was a faith doctor. For, he healed people and used herbs and roots for many illnesses. He would place his finger in a concoction and touch the people and they were later healed.

The next period, I mentioned in this interview is Carrie Lee's adulthood. During this period she grew up to be a woman and married Andrew Davis at age 18, in 1938. One year later, she had a daughter in 1939, Her name was Norma Jean. She was welcome because there were a lot of male-children in the family.

Later, Carrie had seven other children. The first male child was Andrew Davis Jr.

Furthermore, in the interview she stated to me that she owed her long life to two principles, first, to serve God while you are young and the second, is to obey and honor thy parents all the days of your life. Later, in the interview, Mrs. Davis said that children should stay in school and get a good education. My mother would joke that one must get some edmoncation. She stated that once you get an education no one can take that away from you. She emphasized that every child should get an education first.

The intensity of Black people desire for advancement in school was due to the fact that they were denied the opportunity to be educated and during slavery they were legally bar from any learning. The law stated that it was against the law to teach a slave how to read or write. This is why my mother prioritized education first.

Hence, when my mother was young, Blacks had lost the right to vote. For, in the 50's blacks were forced to tip their hats to white people whenever they met them walking. Blacks were not allowed to touch anything in the stores. Blacks had to say sir and yes ma'am to white people no matter how old they were. However after Dr. King helped advance the Black people we can now go anywhere we want. My mother stated that she looked up to leaders of black people, because they were fighting for the advance of all the people. My mother lived a good Christian life. My mother was a believer in God and taught that the maker of mankind had no respect to person, that the sun shines on the good and the evil people.

At this time in the interview my mother discussed the fact that the only provider of education was the church, during the time of my mother's childhood and my early schooling, is a reflection of our oppression. My mother attended school at a church for six years. When she attended school, it was not like today, where children only go to school, but everyone had to work so many days a week in the fields. The school my mother attended was St. Paul Baptist Church School. When I was young I also attended a church School. It was closed to Bethel Baptist Church.

Nevertheless, my entire family was pan of a tradition of being baptized in the Cane River. Thus, my mother was baptized in the Cane River and attended St. Paul Baptist Missionary Church all of her life. All of my family was baptized in the same river and so was my father's family.

However, my mother during this interview spoke of her early childhood as a time when she had very little childhood play time. The only recreation girls of my mothers generation had were children's games. They were allowed to play only on Saturday's. She said, the games they played the most were ring around the roses and miss sally walker. The children would work in the fields with their parents. This was a period in black history, when children were an asset to their parents because they were required to help work the crops. The parents had to be creative, because the children had no television to watch all day.

During the time in the interview I asked my mother about her recent work experiences. The type of work that the masses of black women did, was that of a maid. My mother said, she did babysitting, washing, sweeping, and cleaning for these plantation owners for $50 a week. Black people were exploited for their labor to enrich the white people land share cropping did not end until the 1960's. Blacks were still on farms until the late 1960's.

My Siblings

Due to the fact that Carrie Davis stressed education, all eight of her children were blessed to obtain a college education. The first to go to college was the oldest daughter, who became a school teacher. Three of her children became school teachers. The other five work for some large corporations. The grandchildren are now out of college. There are two out of college. There are two doctors in the family, a pharmacist and a lawyer.

My second oldest brother, Ernest is a graduate of Grambling State University. He played baseball for Grambling. He is a veteran of the Vietnam War. He has two children. Both were adopted when he married his second wife. The oldest, a girl, has now finished college. She graduated from Texas Southern University in Houston Texas. His son is a student at the University of Houston. My younger brother is Gerald Glen. He is a graduate of Southern University in Baton Rouge, Louisiana. He is currently a corporate executive for Chevron, Inc. He has two sons. One of his sons is a graduate of Southern University, and the youngest of his sons attends New York University.

My youngest brother is Gary Wayne. He is also a graduate of Southern University in Baton Rouge, Louisiana. He is now a computer programmer for Northwest Railroad. He has no children. He is a chess master, and a photographer. Gary, has training in Biology. He was once a pre-med honor student while he was at Southern University.

My baby sister, the youngest, Rhonda, is a graduate of Northwestern Statue University. Her daughter is a graduate of Southern University in Baton Rouge and Tulane University Law School in New Orleans, Louisiana.

My oldest sibling is my sister, Norma Jean. She has four children. Her husband is a doctor. Two of her children are doctors. One of her children has a PHD in pharmacy. Her oldest son is an engineer. He was a student of nuclear Engineering at LSU in Baton Rouge, Louisiana.

My next to oldest sibling is my sister, Elise M. Davis. She is married to an accountant. Her four children live in Los Angeles. Two of her children have Bachelor Degrees. They both attended Southern University in Baton Rouge, Louisiana. Her two youngest children also have some college, they are currently seeking degrees.

My oldest brother, the third child, is named after my father. His name is Andrew Jr. He is a High School Coach. He has one son. His son is a graduate of Arizona State University. My brother has been a coach for twenty years. He has influenced a great many young men. He graduated from Southern University in Biology. He has a Master's Degree from Fisk University in Tennessee.

A Short Biography of Leon W. Davis

I will begin by describing the place where I was born, Natchitoches, Louisiana. I am one of eight children. I grew up on farm. I was born in 1947. It was the same year Jackie Robinson entered the major leagues in baseball. I mention this fact because of the influence of sports has had on my family. The fact that my siblings and I were influenced by the fact that blacks were on national television is important because this was the era that Jim Crow smashed.

My father taught us the importance of work. I worked on the farm at the age of nine. I was required to be absent from school twice a week. Those two days that I missed school, I worked on the family farm. I was to have my best record as a student in my first five years at school. Jawanza Kunjufu has stated that the black child have the most success in their first five years of school.

My academic record during my first five years would be of benefit when I enrolled at the University of California Berkeley, later, in my academic career. During my years in high school my academic performance would suffer. I became a juvenile delinquent. I was involved in a gang. We were rebellious against authority in school. We were very interested in females. I was active in sports and I loved to dance. I guess I was the best dancer in the family. I began to notice the emphasis of the society on color during this time. The children in school had a negative concept of black and African people. We were bombarded with ides of f azan and the natives of Africa. We were brainwashed in our studies about black people and slavery. Black was negative, black skin was a curse, your hair was bad if it was nappy.

In 1965, I went off to college to pursue a law degree. I left home alone and was awed by the big city. I remember when I went off to college and returned with ides of Malcolm X. My mother told me not to hate. I told her that black people in the USA loved too much. My mother said that hate would consume you. I told her that in the Bible Solomon had said that it was a time to love, a time to heal and a time to kill.

The summer of 1965 was a historic year because it masked the beginning of the urban uprising that were to span five years of black revolt. The Watts Riot of Los Angeles sparked the revolt of the urban Blacks. Kwame Toure would define the term black power in 1966. Malcolm X had planted the seed of black revolt during his last years. Malcolm was murdered in February of 1965. He had stated that there would be a revolt of black people in the urban ghettoes of America. He said that there was an explosive situation in the major cities, a power-keg that would explode with just a spark. The condition was there for a revolt. He stated that blacks in the city were hostile to the white exploiters of their community. The people who profited from the abject conditions of people caught in the ghetto were white merchants.

My first year, I was introduced to ROTC program. It was mandatory at Southern University that all freshmen and Sophomores be enrolled in ROTC programs. I was a cadet and I was convinced that drill on Monday afternoon was a drag. We even went to the rifle range to practice shooting a rifle. When I heard the student protest against ROTC on campus, I was convinced that it was breeding ground for black soldiers to fight the imperialist wars of America. I made it through the first year with honors. I was given strips in ROTC. I was an honor cadet. I was a squad leader during my second year of ROTC training. The protest against mandatory ROTC training began to surmount. It took on new energy when the Black Power Movement hit the campus. Kwame Toure was on campus in 1955 talking about Vietnam and black power. I read the autobiography of Malcolm X and was transformed into a rebel against the evil white man. I read history written by black men. I started to read black history. In 1967 I was impressed by Kwame Toure's speech on the campus University. He talked about black history and existentialism. That black people should take responsibility for their own lives. That the white man was unable to condemn himself for the treatment had inflicted on people in the third world. Kwame discussed the writings of Franz Fanon, Jean P. Satre, Albert Camus, Nietzche, and Karl Marx in his speech. Later we talked to him at the union where the people were congregating. We talked about Black Power and Kwame explained that the Vietnam War was a racist war. He noted that blacks were being sent to Vietnam in numbers that triple their representation in the population.

The year, 1967 was my junior year at Southern. I was active now in the movement. I was involved in black politics. I campaign for black politicians in Southern Louisiana. I was active in Plaquemine Parish. I was part of a car-pool that carried blacks to the voting polls. During the same year in the city of Baton Rouge, I campaigned for the first city councilman. On campus I boycotted classes and went from classroom to classroom playing tapes of Malcolm X speeches to my fellow students. I was always debating with different students and instructors. I read everything I could find on Africa. I was in conflict with instructors that were conservative and still teaching European Universalism. When I was in a world civilization class I Challenge my history professor that stated that the Egyptian civilization was created by White Europeans.

I also challenged him on his theory that Mesopotamia was before Egyptian civilization. He gave me a D in his class because I would not compromise. Later, I read about the great compromise over slavery during the U.S. Constitutional Debates.

Thus, I decided in 1968 to leave Southern University. I was concerned about the Vietnam War. I had roommates that were hunted by the F.B.I for their stand against the draft. We were informed of the situation of Huey P. Newton and the black Panther Party. We had comrades in Berkeley who were kicked out of Louisiana because of the student strikes. I left for Berkeley to enter a new phase of the Black Revolution.

Bibliography

Carmichael, Stokeley and Charles Hamilton. (1967) *Black Power*, New York: Vintage Books.

Diop, Cheikh, Anta. *The African Origin of Civilization: The Myth or Reality*, Westport, CT, Lawrence Hill and Co., 1974.

Diop, Cheikh, Anta. *An Authentic Anthropology*, New York, Lawrence Hill and Co., 1991.

Kunjufu, Jawanze, *To Be Popular or Smart*, Chicago, Illinois, African American Images, I993.

Malcolm X, *Autobiography of Malcolm X*, New York: Grave Press, 1965.

An interview with Carrie L. Davis by Leon W. Davis, 2001.

This poem is to our ancestors long gone, but now returning

ODE to Marcus

In the wake of Marcus Garvey,
Who stood up for African and said, "I see no nations strong,
I see no kings and queens on a throne,
I see no presidents and men of big affairs,
I will create them"
Marcus who built the black star line
Marcus who organized the universal Negro improvement
association
Marcus who published the Negro world and began the African
Renaissance
And voice appeared
George Padmore and which way Africa communism or
Panafricanism
And W.E.B. Dubois answered Panafricanism
And Garvey sounded out loud
Africa for the African at home and abroad,
While Paul Roberson sang I feel like a motherless child
And Langston Hughes cried out my soul is deep like the rivers
The Nile where greatness appeared through the Eye of Heru
Elijah step forward and said
"Know thy self black man, you are the original man and from you
comes all others
Do for self Noble Drew Ali declared
You are sovereign black man
You are the moor that brought the world out of ignorance to light
For you are the original mason sons of light
Sons and daughters of Kemet
And Kwame Ture said "black power, pan africanism

And John Henry Clark declared pan africanism or perish
And Charellor Williams echoed the rebirth of African civilization
Singing the dance
James Brown, papa got a brand new bag
I am black and proud
Jimmy Hendrick walling voodoo child
Then stepped up to a mountain and chop it down
Up popped Abu Simbel in Kemet, I been there
Bob Marley declared one love, Africa unite
While C. A. Diop writes return to kemet in everything, this is our model
God created the 1st language, hieroglyphics
The 1st sciences, western world, come from our land
Stolen legacy cried GGM James
Greek Philosophy is stolen kemetic deep thought
Dr. Ben Joahanan dug deep in the soil of Kemet and declared the 1st Queens were African
Kemet lives in our mind
God can create the new world
Because the 1st world was our story
Fanon told us
Bring forth the new man
Leave this Europe that is everywhere
Talking of humanity but kills humans everywhere
They find them
Even in the alleys of their own street
My soul is as immense as the universe
But everywhere I am made to feel the humility of the slave
No more
God knows that gods are before alpha and after omega said Khalid Muhammad
Get up black man
There is nothing you cannot do that you have already done.
Iron is strong, but diamonds is the hardest
Kwame Ture says
God will be free, our people will be free

Our struggle is eternal
Never stop struggling
For today the sun is rising
And over the horizon
A new world is being born
Our child cried, all the men are gone
The youth is in jail
Our nation is dying to be born again
Soweto forever
Watts forever
Resist, Resist, Resist
Nothing can stop us
Over the rainbow
The sun rise on New Africa
Deal of the world to us who da da 1st in our of day birth.
II II I 19

Who created the pyramids
And gave the world science, math and all the arts and technology
Then the African world produce, Nkrumah, Kenyatta, Azikwe, Mugabe, Mandela, Amilica Cabreal, Nyerre
And thousands of millions freedom fighters
Up stepped Martin Luther in the USA and Malcolm X fired the first called
Africa must unite,
Came out of the mind of Nkrumah
And we met in 1945 at the 5th Pan African congress
And gave birth to black power, economic, political and cultural power
Ghana was born then Guinea, then Kenya,
Zambia, The Congo Kenya, Tanzania, ect. And ect.
Then we looked and there sat the great beast South Africa
And Mandela rose and says "How can we keep preaching non-violence to an enemy that only responds with violence and death
Biko said "Black consciousness, Amandla!

And children cried power to the people
While Huey P. Newton picked up the gun and step forward
And Declare, in the USA
The black man has no rights
The white man is bound to respect
But the will of the people is stronger than the man's technology
And Bobby Seale said, seize the time!
Up step Rev. Cleage and said we have our own savior
The child of the Black Madonna,
Mugabe stands as the perfect example never bending
Return to the source
Return to the land
Mandela gone
But Winnie lives
Winnie lives
It ain't over
Free the land